Adrian Wynn

I've Got 5 on It

5 Key Pillars That Influence Our Time in Prayer

Edited by Krystal Berry

This book is dedicated to...

To my God who enables me and has so generously chosen me to carry His word to share with this world...

To my wife who has been a constant support and has always cheered for me...

To my children who continue to motivate me...

This is for you.

I love you.

Table of Contents

All I Need Is 5 Minutes

This thought raced through my head as the complications of a dense day increasingly mounted against me. The workday began on a sour note and the problems just seemed to be pouring into my day. Relentless… is probably a vast understatement to describe the way things had bombarded my space. And as the time ticked past the noon hour, I managed to mumble, again, through the chaos of the day, "All I need is 5 minutes!"

I'd had enough! I secured my phone inside of my desk and stood up to make my escape. While walking down the hall, my mind was moving at super speed thinking about what I needed to do during my 5-minute escape from the chaos that invaded my day. *What will I do? How will I spend this time?* And it was there… in that place… at that moment, that God arrested me and gave me instructions as to what I needed to do with my next 5 minutes. He wanted me to spend time alone with Him. There was to be no interruption, no invasion and no interference. God literally wanted my entire 5 minutes, and He got it!

After spending those 5 minutes talking with God, there was a completely different feeling that I walked away with. It wasn't an unusual calm. It wasn't a fierceness. It wasn't empowerment.

It was a thirst for *more* time… *uninterrupted* time alone with Him.

The world around us moves at such a rapid pace that we often times forget to be good stewards of two of the most important things that we have access to: our relationship with God and our time. The absolute best and brightest gift that heaven had to offer was given by God in exchange for our salvation. Because of the love that God commended towards us, we have access to the grace wherein we stand. Far too often, however, we seemingly forget that it is in Him that we live, move, and have our being. In the strategic planning of our day, we fail to invest an appropriate amount of energy and effort into the cultivation of a better relationship with God. Ironically, we reserve time to develop our horizontal relationships, and we do this at our own peril, seeming to miss the constant invitation of God… summoning us closer to himself.

And *time*-- another amazing gift that we have access to is very much a limited commodity. We are all allotted a certain amount of time to make an impact on this world. We do not have the convenience of adding units to our lifetime account. We are given what we have and we must be careful not to become so consumed with the menial things of life, that we fail to prioritize our time and give God the time that He deserves.

Sadly, we often think that in order to give God what He is deserving of, we must sacrifice the greater portion of our day. God truly is deserving of most of, if not all, of our time. But in order to develop and cultivate a relationship with God, though He doesn't ask for all of you time, He does ask for some of it. In one of the most critical moments of the life of Jesus, He asks the disciples, after He came to the disciples and found them asleep, He said to Peter, *"What? Could you not watch with Me one hour?"-Matthew 26:40 (NKJV)* These were men that had walked in the shadows and footsteps of Jesus for three years and He simply requested an hour and they were unable to stay awake.

In this age of social media, if I were to tally up and account for every moment of engagement, I am sure I lose at least an hour each day just checking notifications or interacting with my peers via various platforms. The postmodern lifestyle is by and large not designed to carve out space that, to the naked eye, seems to be unproductive. I, however, contend that any and every moment you spend with God will be some of the most fulfilling, rewarding, and productive moments of your entire existence. There is a richly deep benefit to having a one-on-one audience with the Creator of the entire universe. The ability to petition the same God that thrust the world into existence with the spoken Word of His mouth is not to be overlooked, taken lightly, or taken for granted.

In light of understanding and establishing how big God is, how He wields an unimaginable amount of power through the entire universe, how He is the sole proprietor of the heavens and the earth, and how He is the source from which everything that ever was began, I'd like you to consider this question: *is He worth 5 minutes of your time?*

Before you jump in feet first, consider that if it were as easy as it sounds to pray a prayer that moves heaven and earth, for a full 5-uniterrupted minutes, then I, most likely, would not be writing this book. At initial consideration, 5 minutes seems like a very small amount of time to spend in prayer. The truth, however, is that many people will struggle with filling a 5-minute time span of prayer without asking God for the same things over and over again. Because of the perpetual movement of our lives, most of us have been so conditioned to remain in motion that we find it to be a significant challenge to pause for just 5 minutes and have a direct conversation with the same God who we refer to as Lord.

If we were to be forthcoming, many of us would have to acknowledge that when we pray, after we have concluded our time of asking God for all of the blessings that we desire, most of us struggle to continue with anything meaningful in our time of prayer. In fact, even as we are making our requests known to God, sometimes, we may struggle with not knowing exactly what we ought to ask for. For that reason, God has setup a divine appointment between you and this book in order to give you a very practical roadmap to help you in your time of prayer. This book is not just about the importance of spending time in prayer. It is also a guide to help you jumpstart your prayer life and, in turn, begin to cultivate an amazing relationship with God our Father.

To give you context for this book, it's inspired by the 5 major pillars that prop up the lives of just about all people. Regardless to race, creed, religious affiliation, generation, or gender, there are 5 primary pillars that support our lives. These 5 pillars are essential to our understanding and most importantly to shape our time and prayers to God. These pillars include: **The Physical** (Body), **The Social** (Relationships), **The Mental** (Mind), **The Financial** (Money) and **The Emotional** (Soul.) Throughout the remainder of this book, I will give you basic principles to help you jumpstart your prayer life relative to these very specific areas. This book is not an exhaustive guide. It is designed to be a starting point for anyone that is trying to start or strengthen their prayer life. As we take this journey together, it is my prayer that you not only engage this book, but that you employ its strategies in your daily life and develop a prayer life that draws you closer in your relationship with God.

Can you spare 5 more minutes?

Chapter 1:
The Physical

Do you not know that your body is a temple of the Holy Spirit who is within you, whom you have [received as a gift] from God, and that you are not your own [property]? You were bought with a price [you were actually purchased with the precious blood of Jesus and made His own]. So then, honor and glorify God with your body.

-1 Corinthians 6:19-20 (AMP)

Father, cleanse your temple...

You have been placed in charge of one of the most precious things ever created. From the beginning of time, God saw fit that, at this particular point in history, your life is needed. The gifts, skills, wisdom, and problem-solving abilities your life brings to the world are necessary for this moment. God has uniquely designed your body as the vehicle that He wants to use to bring your contributions to this world. We have been made stewards over that vehicle and been trusted by God to keep it in the best possible condition. This then requires an understanding that our bodies do not belong to us. We are simply stewards of this body, which has been lent to us for the primary work of service to God our Father.

Our bodies could be viewed as Kingdom company vehicles. They are the property, of God, to be used for the purposes of God, however the preservation of these vehicles is a shared responsibility. God gives us a life, a measure of health and strength, and instructions on how to keep this vehicle running at optimum level.

So, what is it exactly that does damage to these God-given vehicles? One of the most devastating ways that we damage our vehicle is through sin. Sin does not discriminate. It is something that every child of God must deal with...*for all have sinned and fallen short of the glory of God, -Romans* 3:23 (NIV). Even with our very best efforts, there are times that we will still fall into sin. The grace of God, however, is so sufficient for us that our Father *is faithful and just to forgive us of our sins and cleanse us from all unrighteousness* -1 John 1:9b (NIV). And the word of God gives us the assurance that God is more than able to cleanse us from the stain and residue of bad decisions and ungodly living practices. When we have committed sins of omission (the things we didn't do) and commission (the things we did do), we have caused the vehicle of our giftings to become dirtied and contaminated.

There is a real responsibility that we have to ensure that the presentation of what God has created for us, to deliver to the world, is not disregarded based on the lack of care that we have exhibited in our stewardship. Therefore, when we pray, we should ask according to the word of God: *Father cleanse your temple.* By doing so, we acknowledge the role we play as stewards of the vehicle, the responsibility we take for contaminating the vehicle, the ability of God to cleanse it and make it suitable for His use once again, and lastly we acknowledge that we were not designed to make this journey alone.

Father, let your Holy Spirit dwell in this temple...

Our bodies are not only our vehicle, but they are also the space where the Holy Spirit dwells. When Jesus departed from the earth, He instructed those present to wait in expectation for the Comforter, the Holy Spirit, who would reside on the inside of us. The Spirit serves as a guide, an encourager, an accountability system, a source of supernatural and divine power and even as a protector. Because of this, we want the spirit of God to dwell within us. The journey of life quickly becomes overwhelming and we quickly lose our bearings when we attempt to navigate life and its circumstances without the aid of the Holy Spirit.

When we operate with a cleansed temple, we should have no reservations about asking God to allow His spirit to dwell within us. The word of God reminds us that *the wicked flee when no one pursues them, but the righteous are as bold as a lion -Proverbs 28:1 (AMP).* I believe that in most cases, the inverse is also true. When we have failed to ask God to cleanse us, we are reluctant to invite the Holy Spirit into a place that we know is cluttered and filled with the evidence of our disobedience to God's instructions for our lives. When we invite the Holy Spirit into our lives, we have access to the power that God gives us to make an impact in the world. *But truly I am full of power by the spirit of The Lord, and of justice and might, to declare to Jacob his transgression and to Israel his sin -Micah 3:8 (AMP).*

This revelation is one that will drastically change your existence. We are powerful beings when we operate under the authority of God and in the power of His Holy Spirit. This revelation helps us to not just take life as it comes, but it empowers us to always be in purpose and not be crushed under the weight of current circumstances.

Asking the Holy Spirit to dwell within us is a simple request with a complex construct. When we invite the Spirit of God to reside in us, we relinquish the rights to dictate what we release and reserve access to. We cannot release Him to dwell in our financial status but reserve the right to make financial decisions apart from His will. We cannot release Him to dwell in our assignment as parents but reserve the right to lead them down a path that does not honor God. We cannot release Him to justify us and vindicate us from the attacks of our enemies yet reserve the right to take out vengeance when an opportunity presents itself.

If we are to invite Him into our lives, we should give Him free reign over every detail that concerns us! There is an amazing freedom we can rest in when we allow the Spirit of God to dwell in us. *Now the Lord is the Spirit; and where the Spirit of the Lord is, there is freedom -2 Corinthians 3:17 (NIV).* When we spend time with God, in prayer, one of the most necessary petitions that we should make is...*Father, let your Holy Spirit dwell in me.* Without this perspective, we are simply on a road trip without a destination, without a compass, without a GPS system, without protection and without anything to fuel the fire that we need to propel our engines forward into destiny and purpose.

Father, build your temple...

Divine health and healing are available to the believer. Through the power of prayer, we have the right and privilege to request that God, the owner and creator of our bodies, would strengthen them for the purposes in which we have been designed for. As a believer, we can pray for supernatural healing of all diseases, relief from all pains and deliverance from sicknesses. Again, this space in our prayers goes back to the basic understanding that our bodies belong to God. If we treat our bodies as if they belong to God regularly, we are well within the plan and will of God, according to the scriptures, to submit it back to Him for repairs.

Over time, it is inevitable that our bodies will experience wear and tear, and this is perfectly okay. There is a vast difference, however, between our bodies being worn because we've put in work for the Kingdom, and our bodies being worn because we've mishandled and abused them for our own pleasures and purposes.

Here is where our prayer life and practical life must move hand-in-hand. We cannot reasonably expect God to consistently repair our broken bodies that have been broken down due to our broken obedience. If we have an expectation of God to heal our body's dis-ease, it would only be right that God have an expectation of us that we would do with our bodies what He has requested.

The power of prayer does not cancel out the consequences of willful disobedience. This part of the prayer journey is not just about "fixing" pain and disease. It also applies to asking God to build up our temple so that we don't fall victim to our own flesh. As God is building our temples, He is not only repairing those parts that have been broken down and damaged over time, but I believe that He has the power to repair the "gates" to our temples as well.

Our gates play an intricate role in the objective of sustaining our temple. It is our responsibility, through action, to monitor and maintain the gates that allow passage into our temples. It is our responsibility, in prayer, to seek to give attention and expectation to the things that build us up opposed to the things that cause cracks and vulnerability in our temples.

Now when the evening had come, they brought to Him many who were demon-possessed. And He cast out the spirits with a word and healed all who were sick. That it might be fulfilled which was spoken by Isaiah the

prophet, saying: "He Himself took our infirmities and
bore our sicknesses."
-Matthew 8:16-17(AMP).

A precedent has been set for us waking in divine healing. On numerous occasions, we read about men and women of God, used in scripture, to heal those who were sick among them. We saw this play out the more in the life of Jesus. Whether it was because He was moved with compassion for them or if it were so that the words of the prophet would be fulfilled, we can recall Jesus healing people that were struggling with sickness. According to the plan of God, for all of our lives, we are to use the life of Jesus as a template, an example or pattern for how we are to live and move throughout our journey. If Jesus has a problem with sickness dominating the lives of those that surrounded Him, we should have the same perspective. *"And these signs shall follow them that believe; In my name shall they cast out devils; they shall speak with new tongues; They shall take up serpents; and if they drink any deadly thing, it shall not hurt them; they shall lay hands on the sick, and they shall recover"-Mark 16:17-18 (KJV).*

The scriptures give us a syllabus for life. Not only do we find encouragement, peace, correction, and hope in them, but we also find instructions. When there are sick among us, according to scripture, we are to *call for the elders of the church; and let the pray over them, anointing them with oil in the name of Jesus: and the PRAYER OF FAITH shall save the sick, and the Lord*

19

shall raise them up; and if they have committed sins they shall be forgiven them -James 5:14-15 (AMP). Therefore, when we pray, let us petition God to build our temple.

Father, make my temple worth its cost...

One of the most heart wrenching and routinely overlooked realities, concerning our physical bodies (temples), is we, all too often, treat it as if it costs nothing. Perhaps it is because we were not the ones responsible for paying the costs involved. It is indeed a gross case of negligence to haphazardly handle the limited commodity of our bodies without taking time to reflect on and acknowledge the tremendous costs associated with being redeemed. The astonishing truth is that with all of our flaws, inconsistencies, mishaps, and missteps, God still looks at our lives and sees an enormous value in us. There is layer after layer of disobedience, disregard, doubt, deception, disrespect, and defiance, yet God sees enough in us to decide that we were worth redeeming. *Christ hath redeemed us from the curse of the law, being made a curse for us: for it is written, Cursed is everyone that hangeth on a tree: - Galatians 3:13 (AMP).* God saw so much value in your temple, He paid for it with the precious life and blood of Jesus. And this was the rarest and most precious gift heaven had to offer: the life of the unblemished lamb of God. Without a hesitation, God willingly offered His son in exchange for the eternal security of you and me.

In most cases, there is a difference between the cost of a thing and the value of that same thing. Just because something has a certain price, it does not always mean the cost actually matches the value. The interesting thing about this whole scenario is that what make us valuable are the things that God has put inside of us. God had a choice! Those very same gifts, skills, talents and experiences could have very easily been distributed into another vessel. Every single thing that God has deposited into us raises the value of who we are to match the cost of what He paid to redeem us. Make no mistake about it: you are valuable to God--so valuable are you that *He has created you only a little lower than the angels -Psalms 8:5a (NIV).*

God has entrusted us with dominion over all of the works of His hands. That amount of trust speaks to the level of gifting to which God has deposited into you. Everything that God has created is subject to your authority--what an awesome gesture of affirmation and confirmation of value from the proprietor of the universe.

It is absolutely possible, perhaps, that we have not accurately assessed what we mean to God. We may have misjudged what we mean to Him-- especially considering that He gave the absolute best of Heaven in exchange for us. Therefore, my time in prayer must include a request that God would allow my temple to continue to be worth its cost. God must get value from His investment in my life and body. Ironically, without His assistance and protection, this amazingly complicated body, with its countless blood vessels, arteries, organs, muscles, and bones, becomes nothing more than a housing unit for a soul that has not reached its purpose or full potential. Always remember to ask of our Father to make our temple worth its costs...*in Jesus' name.*

Father, get glory from this temple...

It has been established, that our bodies are in fact the transportation for our souls. Our souls are to reflect the nature of our Father who created us. Our bodies are to help us carry out the assignments of our lives. We've used, as a tool for illustration, our bodies being likened to company cars. God has created our bodies uniquely to accomplish our specific purpose in life. This means that our company car (body) is specifically fashioned to accomplish the task that will bring attention, adoration, praise, honor and distinction to our Father who has created it. In other words, the primary responsibility of this body that we have been blessed with is to use it in every way possible to bring glory to God.

There are so many different ways that we can regularly leverage this temple that we call a body. It should be a priority that we leverage it in as many ways as possible to bring God glory. For example: physically, we can pray that our hands are lifted to worship Him, or our hands are used to be a point of contact, for the sick among us, as we pray that they recover. Perhaps we pray that our legs are used to take us to areas to serve the disenfranchised, the debilitated, the disabled, the desperate and the downtrodden. Our lips can be used to speak well of our Father so that all may come to know how great He is. The eyes that we have been given can be used to see good in others when most people only see the bad. Using our arms to embrace a brother, sister or child that is wrestling with depression, anxiety, or discontentment is also a way to leverage the body that we have been given to bring God glory. What a shame it would be to gladly take the provisions of a body from our Father and use it as we see fit as opposed to using it in the prescribed manner that the Father desires and commands.

But you shall receive power when the Holy Spirit has come upon you; and you shall be witnesses to Me in Jerusalem, and in all Judaea and Samaria, and to the end of the earth. -Acts 1:8 (NIV).

Serving as witnesses to our God is the best and primary way to honor Him. We already have the Holy Spirit residing inside of us; therefore, we have access to the power of God. Still we must possess more than just spiritual power. We also need physical strength and stamina if we are to carry out the mission of being witnesses for God all around the world. Furthermore, our temples are a visual demonstration of the power of the God that we represent. It is important that we look as if things are well with us, but it is also important that things are *actually* well with us. When we commit to doing what is necessary to maintain our temples, we are then able to leverage our bodies to ensure that God gets the glory out of our temples.

It never ceases to amaze me how we can approach the church with a certain reverence and respect yet disregard our bodies as if they are not also the houses of the Lord. If we would begin to petition God, specifically, in prayer, to get glory out of our temples, it would change our level of awareness: where we take our temples, what we deposit into them, what we allow to come out of them and the way in which we offer them back to God. As children of God, we must always be acutely aware that during our journey here on earth, as well as at the conclusion thereof, we must offer this temple back to God. Therefore, when we pray, let us be consistent and intentional regarding our petition for God, to please Him, and so that He may get glory out from our temples.

Can you spare 5 more minutes?

Pillar in Practice:
The Physical

1 Corinthians 6:19-20 AMP

Whether this becomes your personal devotion, or you choose to complete this work in a group setting, these after-chapter lessons seek to assist you in applying what you have read. It is our Father's desire that we not simply be hearers (and seers) of the word, but that we become *doers* of His word!

Let's do the work!

KEY TRUTHS
1. Pray that God would CLEANSE His temple!
2. Pray that The Holy Spirit would DWELL in you!
3. Pray that His temple would be BUILT UP (strengthened)!
4. Pray that His temple would be WORTH the price that was paid for it!
5. Pray the His temple would bring Him GLORY!

CLEANSE YOUR TEMPLE

The analogy is that our body is the equivalent of a company car. We must understand that our body does not belong in whole to us. We are simply stewards of bodies lent to us to use in the service of the Lord.

Do you not know that your body is a temple of the Holy Spirit who is within you, whom you have (received as a gift) from God, and that you are not your own (property)? You were bought with a price (you were actually purchased with the precious blood of Jesus and made His own). So then, honor and glorify God with your body.
- 1 Corinthians 6:19-20 (AMP)

HOLY SPIRIT, DWELL IN THIS TEMPLE

When Jesus departed from earth, the Holy Spirit came and began to fill all who desired and requested it. But the Holy Spirit will not dwell in an unclean temple. Therefore, when we have cleansed our temple, we should pray that The Holy Spirit would dwell in us.

But as for me, I am filled with power, with the Spirit of the Lord, and with justice and might, to declare to Jacob his transgression, to Israel his sin.
-Micah 3:8 (NIV)

All of them were filled with the Holy Spirit and began to speak in other tongues as the Spirit enabled them.
-Acts 2:4 (NIV)

BUILD UP MY TEMPLE

Divine health and healing are available to the believer. We have the power, through prayer, to request that God would strengthen our bodies. We can pray for supernatural healing of all diseases, relief from all pains, and deliverance from sicknesses, and we can receive these things if they be in accordance with the will of God.

When evening came, many who were demon-possessed were brought to him, and he drove out the spirits with a word and healed all the sick. This was to fulfill what was spoken through the prophet Isaiah: "He took up our infirmities and bore our diseases."
- Matthew 8:16-17 (NIV)

And these signs shall follow them that believe; In my name shall they cast out devils; they shall speak with new tongues; They shall take up serpents; and if they drink any deadly thing, it shall not hurt them; they shall lay hands on the sick, and they shall recover.
-Mark 16:17-18 (KJV)

MAKE MY TEMPLE WORTH ITS COST

God sees so much value in your life and in your temple that when Jesus was crucified, he carried away every sin and sickness. He paid for your temple with the precious life/blood of Jesus Christ. That was an expensive price to pay, but God valued you enough to spare no expense. Pray that God would make your temple worthy of what it cost Him to redeem it.

Christ redeemed us from the curse of the law by becoming a curse for us, for it is written: "Cursed is everyone who is hung on a pole."
- Galatians 3:13 (NIV)
Surely he hath borne our griefs and carried our sorrows: yet we did esteem him stricken, smitten of God, and afflicted. But he was wounded for our transgressions, he was bruised for our iniquities: the chastisement of our peace was upon him; and with his stripes we are healed.
- Isaiah 53:4-5 (NIV)

GET GLORY FROM THIS TEMPLE

The primary responsibility of this physical body, God has lent to us, is for us to use it to bring Him Glory.

But you shall receive power when the Holy Spirit has come upon you; and you shall be my witnesses to Me in Jerusalem, and in all Judea and Samaria, and to the ends of the earth.
-Acts 1:8 (NIV)

Chapter Two:

The Social

As iron sharpens iron so a man sharpens the countenance of his friend.

-Proverbs 27:17 (NKJV)

Father, help me to identify my own worth...

My prayers are not prayed in a vacuum. I pray at the level of my understanding and I pray from my life's vantage point. It is vitally important to not only understand my positioning in prayer, but I must also understand my worth. Specifically, when I am praying about my social interactions and social circles-- I need to understand my value to God as well as my potential value to others. The valuation that others place on me is not necessarily something that I can control, however, it is something that I must be acutely aware of. My worth was determined when God decided that my life and eternity was worth sacrificing the life of His only son in exchange for my own. God knows my worth, but when I go to Him in prayer, does my assessment of my worth match His? I've heard it said in many settings and on many occasions, "We date at the level of our confidence."

And this "dating" is not simply about physical intimacy. We court potential friendships and intimate relationships based on our level of confidence as well. Sometimes, we make the mistake of courting relationships to achieve a level of self-worth, but that is worth defined by the way someone who did not create you has come to view you. That's entirely too much power to give to someone who is not responsible for your existence. God's tells Jeremiah, *"before I formed you in the womb I knew you, before you were born, I set you apart..." -1:5 (NIV)*. This is that our worth was already defined when God decided that He would provide life to the women who carried us in their wombs. And it is our responsibility to ensure that the One who created us is honored before we even cultivate other relationships.

Not only do we honor our creator by knowing that our worth comes from Him, but we also keep His commandment. The previous 5 minutes forced us to recall the care of our temples. And the truth is, if we don't value our temples, we won't respect them. It's the same socially: you must value yourself before you can value others. We have a responsibility to speak life into ourselves. Many times, we spend so much time being self-critical and talking about ourselves in a negative way that we create habits of not seeing the good in anything we do. We begin to question existence and purpose when it has already been established by a sovereign God. And valuing yourself is not an option according to the word of God; it's a commandment. Paul tells the church at Rome, *"But God commendeth his love toward us, in that while we were yet inners, Christ died for us" -Romans 5:8 (KJV)*. It's a beautiful perspective that God didn't wait until we had everything "together," but while we were in our dirtiest and most detestable states of being, He decided, even in our mess, we were still worth saving! So, when we sing Anthony Brown's "Worth," it's a direct correlation to the value God has placed on our lives. To know God's love for us is to know our own personal value and to know our personal value in Christ is to know God's love for us.

Father, help me identify the worth of others...

One of the mistakes we often make, when meeting someone, is our greetings to one another. Our first questions are not always, "how was your day," "are you feeling well today," "has anyone hugged you today," or "do you feel loved today?" Many times, when we meet someone the conversation is: "what's your name and what do you do?" And unfortunately, many of us will cultivate opinions of others once we find out what is that they do for a living. This then relegates the person's worth to what they do and not who they are. And the reality is, that same perspective applies to us.

Not only do we have a commandment to know our self-worth, but we've been commanded to value the worth of others. *Love the Lord your God with all your heart and with all your soul and with all your mind and with all your strength. The second is this: Love your neighbor as yourself" -Mark 12: 30-31(NIV).* Here, Jesus gives clear instructions in scripture. When we truly want God to bless our social relationships, we don't mistreat others because we 1- know the worth of God, 2-we know the worth of Christ's life in saving ours and 3- we want others to be treated as well as we desire to be treated.

In moments of meditation, it is crucial for us to pray and ask God to reveal to us not simply where we haven't valued ourselves, but where we have failed to value others. Perhaps our social circles don't honor the commandment given to us. Involving ourselves in circles full of gossip are not edifying to the call to others that God has placed on our lives. The desire to diminish the value of others to make ourselves appear valuable is not to have the mind of Christ. But our prayers must reflect our love for Christ, ourselves, and then for others. This will be visible through our actions. When we pray that God would allow us to see the value in ourselves, we, in turn, value him. Afterall, Jesus speaks in the book of Matthew, *"...Truly I tell you, whatever you did for one of the least of these brothers of Mine, you did for Me"*- *Matthew 25:40 (NIV)*.

Father, help me to sharpen others as I am sharpened by them...

Most of us struggle with relationships because we don't handle them with care. There are a number of classes that we matriculate through, during our educational careers, and we are taught how to have a command of the English language along with at least one additional dialect. We are taught historical facts that are important to our history as a country. We are taught how to navigate algebraic equations and how to solve for "x." With all of the important lessons that we are taught, unfortunately, we missed one of the most vital lessons that relates to our success. We are not formally taught how to elect, engage in, or manage relationships. The tragedy of this reality is that most of us have to learn how to navigate relationships through trial and error, and there are usually more errors than there are healthy and thriving relationships.

Everyone that we meet is a relationship waiting to happen. The word of God reminds, *"And let us consider how we may spur one another on toward love and good deeds, not giving up meeting together, as some are in the habit of doing, but encouraging one another—and all the more as you see the Day approaching" -Hebrews 10:24-25 NIV*. On a daily basis, we encounter dozens of people that could be a part of beneficial relationships for us to engage in. There is no such thing as a neutral relationship. In every relationship, we are either being moved in a positive direction because of it or a negative direction. Whether it is positive or a negative, there is something to be learned from it. Still, according to the word of God, being in a positive relationship will cause you to be "sharpened." One of the biggest gifts of relationship is that they have the potential to help us become better than we currently are. When it comes to relationships or relational issues, our prayers are many times either tailored to intimate relationships or focused on repairing fractured relationships. Both of these areas are bettered by our attention to them, in prayer, but it is vital that we also include making petitions to God about the relationships that we need to be in to sharpen us.

Countless numbers of books, classes, webinars, and coaches exist with the sole purpose of helping us to grow and develop. People invest countless dollars into various avenues to attempt to jumpstart their personal growth. What would happen if we invested that same energy, in prayer, for wisdom about relationships? Prayer is the place of exchange between heaven and earth. Through prayer, God can reveal the qualities, the makeup, the personality type, the background or even the future assignment of the people that I need to be connected to in this season of my life. Don't be mistaken: every relationship is not for every season. A relationship out of season, can throw off the trajectory of your growth, and subsequently cause regress opposed to progress. Wisdom, however, revealed through prayer, gives us insight not only regarding who we should pursue relationships with, but it also tells us when such relationships are beneficial and when they would be burdensome.

And those relationships are to be handled carefully. 'Iron sharpens iron,' literally suggests that there are mutual benefits to these relationships. Be prayerful that you are giving as much as you get in relationships. Also pray that you are not being drained in a relationship where a mutual benefit does not exist. Pray that your conversation is always seasoned with grace and that your words, rooted in the word of God, are able to sharpen your brother or sister.

Can you spare 5 more minutes?

Pillar in Practice:

The Social

Proverbs 27:17 (AMP)

MOST OF US STRUGGLE WITH RELATIONSHIPS BECAUSE WE DON'T DO THEM RIGHT! There is not a class that teaches us how to do relationships properly, and, as a consequence, we usually fumble through life until we figure out some way to get them right. The problem is we usually mess up quite a few things along the way. Every person that we meet is a relationship waiting to happen. Deductively, it is conceivable that one of the gifts of relationships is to make us sharper. Every interaction that we have with others is education in and of itself. Each time that we encounter others we rub together like two iron blades.

Let's do the work!

KEY TRUTHS
1. God help me to identify my worth!
2. God help me to identify the worth of others!
3. God help me to sharpen others as I am sharpened by them!

HELP ME IDENTIFY MY WORTH

As we engage God in prayer, we should ask that He would help us to be aware of and convinced of what people get when they get us. We have all been uniquely fashioned by God to meet a specific need in this earth. YOU BRING SOMETHING TO THE TABLE.

Before I formed you in the womb, I knew you, before you were born, I set you apart
- Jeremiah 1:5 (NIV)

But God commendeth his love toward us, in that while we were yet inners, Christ died for us.
-Romans 5:8 (KJV)

HELP ME TO IDENTIFY THE WORTH OF OTHERS

Jesus selects 12 disciples--not based on their status, accomplishments, or financial capabilities. He selects these men based on what the combination of His life and their life would produce. When we pray for this area of our lives, we should pray that we would not take lightly what others bring to our lives.

He who walks with wise men will be wise, But the companion of fools will be destroyed. - Proverbs 13:20 (NKJV)

Love the Lord your God with all your heat and with all your soul and with all your mind and with all your strength. The second is this: Love your neighbor as yourself
-Mark 12:30-31 (NIV)

A friend loves at all times, And a brother is born for adversity.
- Proverbs 17:17 (NKJV)

...Truly I tell you, whatever you did for one of the least of these brothers and sisters of Mine, you did for Me.
- Matthew 25:40 (NIV)

HELP ME TO SHARPEN AND TO BE SHARPENED

Sharpen: to make or cause a person to be keen in perception, quick witted, or full of energy, or to awaken the mind of another. In this area, we should ask God to expose us to people we can be sharpened by, and people we can likewise sharpen.

And let us consider one another in order to stir up love and good works, not forsaking the assembling of ourselves together, as is the manner of some, but exhorting one another, and so much the more as you see the Day approaching.

`- Hebrews 10:24-25 (NKJV)

Chapter Three:

The Mental

Do not conform to the pattern of this world but be transformed by the renewing of your mind. Then you will be able to test and approve what God's will is--His good, pleasing and perfect will

-Romans 12:2 (NIV)

Father, guard the gates to my mind...

We are products of our thoughts. Bearing this in mind, it is important to monitor and guard what we allow to enter into our minds. Everything that comes through our gates is a seed planted in the grounds of our mind. We have two primary gates to our minds: the eyes and the ears. It is necessary that we are proactively monitoring what we see and hear in an effort to guard our gates. We are literally instructed, through scripture, to be the watchmen of our own gates. Consider this: we have gates to our physical bodies and the health of our total physical person is dependent on our intake. The same can be said for our minds. Solomon suggests to us, *"For as he thinketh in his heart, so is he..." -Proverbs 23:7 (KJV)*. If how I think determines who I am, then my desire, as a believer should be to have the mind of Christ. This is why Paul admonishes the Philippian church to, *"let this mind be in you which was also in Christ Jesus..." -Philippians 2:5 (KJV)*.

Guarding the gates of our minds must begin in prayer. Communication is what will affect those gates in a positive or negative way. We feed our spirit man through what we see, hear, and say. Between televisions, radio, social media, and conversations that we encounter, during our day, our spirits are exposed to so much that could harm us. Therefore, beginning our days with time in devotion is not optional if we are to keep watch over our gates. And in our humanity, we don't always get it right. But every day we are alive we have an opportunity to get things right. We also guard our gates by constantly reading the word of God. This is why Paul says, *"whatever you have learned or received or heard from me or seen in me- put it into practice"-Philippians 4:9a (NIV)*. This is that we cannot simply see what to do, or hear what to do, we have to be doers of all that we have been commanded.

The product of obediently guarding our gates is detailed in scripture: peace. Peace is the end result of guarded gates. Paul finishes off his statement to the Philippian church by praying that the God of peace be with them. And it's the words of Isaiah the prophet that support the reality of God's peace going with us, *"you will keep him in perfect peace, Whose mind is stayed on You, Because he trusts in You" -Isaiah 26:3(NIV)*. What an exchange! Keeping watch over the gates of my mind allows me to experience the peace of God that will surpass all understanding!

Father, guard the grounds of my mind...

Have you ever started your day with devotion to God? You have a song of praise on your lips and in your heart, and you are ready to take on the day! You literally "woke up with your mind stayed on Jesus." But despite your preparation, you arrive at work, or at that meeting, or you are traveling on the highway and that one person just takes you completely out of your mood. This doesn't put your salvation in question, but it does suggest that even when giving our best effort, there are some things that get beyond the gates of our minds and make its way into the grounds (battlegrounds) of our mind.

Whether it is by way of our subconsciousness or we are spontaneously privy to a form of communication, it is necessary that the grounds of our minds are guarded. We should pray that God would guard our grounds so that anything that is not like Him will not be able to stay, grow, or produce fruit. Everything that gets in does not have to stay in! Just as our bodies are to His glory, so it should be with our thoughts! Our thoughts must belong to the Lord. The word of God reminds us, *"casting down arguments and every high thing that exalts itself against the knowledge of God, bringing every thought into captivity to the obedience of Christ," -2 Corinthians 10:5 (NIV)*. This is what we've been called to do!

The practical piece to this is also found in the word of God: *"Finally, brethren, whatsoever things are true, whatsoever things are honest, whatsoever things are just, whatsoever things are pure, whatsoever things are lovely, whatsoever things are of good report; if there be any virtue, and if there be any praise, think on these things" - Philippians 4:8 (KJV).* It's imperative that our minds have a particular focus. The ground of our minds is where thoughts can take root to our hearts. We have heard it time and time again that an idle mind can be satan's playground. And those silent and motionless grounds of the mind must be dedicated to the thoughts of Christ. If not, our unfocused mind becomes a battlefield because sin begins in the mind. We will begin to dedicate that space to our own selves and seek to please us. This puts the mind in cooperation with the flesh. And soon, we begin to experience war with our flesh because our minds have not been properly renewed. Devotional moments are critical to having the mind of Christ because our first offering should be to dedicate our thoughts to the glory of our God. Our thoughts have to be centered on what is true, honest, just, pure, lovely, of good report, etc.

If we can do this daily, our actions will also be reflective of what is in our mind. Seasoned saints would always say that when the grounds of our minds have not been guarded, it doesn't matter what we propose in action. Their suggestion is that 'new hands will go where old hands have been. New feet will go where old feet have been' if there is no real change or focus on the inside—*in the mind.* And when we pray to God, to guard the grounds of our minds, scripture tells us *"... on the good ground are they, which in an honest and good heart, having heard the word, keep it, and bring forth fruit with patience" -Luke 8:15 (KJV).* The product of a guarded mind ensures that not only do we hear the word, not only will we be able to keep the word, but that we will manifest fruit(positivity) in our lives. Prayer and intercession allow only what is pure and what is good to occupy the grounds of our minds. When everything around us seems to be in chaos, it is then our responsibility to take on the posture of prayer and intercession to ensure that the grounds of our minds are kept safe.

Father, guard the gifts in my mind…

Gifted minds tend to overthink which causes overreaction. Our mind is the place of exchange and development. Information goes in, it is developed, and it is expelled in a variety of different ways. What we speak and what we do is how the information is expelled. We should pray that God would guard the gifts that He has given us that begin in our minds. We pray for those gifts to be guarded because they have been given and ought to be set aside for His glory. They are not set aside for us to engage in anxiety with them. The word of God admonishes us to be anxious for nothing. And through prayer and time with God, the peace that has been promised consumes our thoughts. That peace consumes our emotions. That same peace will consume our thinking and it prevents anxiety from taking over. So, to overthink and overreact exposes a dependency on ourselves and not on who we have asked and trusted to guard the gifts so freely given to us.

Gifted minds also find trouble in conforming. Matthew's gospel reminds us of exactly who we are, *"Ye are the light of the world. A city that is set on a hill cannot be hid. Neither do men light a candle, and put it under a bushel, but on a candlestick; and it giveth light unto all that are in the house. Let your light so shine before men, that they may see your good works, and glorify your Father which is in heaven" -Matthew 5:14-16 (KJV).*

Asking God to guard this is essential to carrying out what He has assigned to our lives. The gifts of the mind must be guarded because satan will use others to attempt to influence us and adjust our thinking which affects how our light shines. Guarded gifts of the mind won't yield to their own understanding. Guarded minds won't have a desire to conform to the understanding of others, but it will conform to the thoughts of Christ. The truth is that total surrender to God modifies our thinking and guards the gates, the grounds, and the gifts of the mind for the complete glory of God.

Our prayers should always be that in having guarded gates, grounds, and gifts of the mind, that what we do is consistently to the glory of God. When our motives are pure, God will allow what He has guarded to blossom and we will be able to share, what began in the mind, in a more expressive way: *"A man's gift makes*

room for him, And brings him before great men"-
Proverbs 18:16 (NKJV).

When God so graciously provides us with a gift, our prayer for that gift to be guarded is timely. And the truth of God's word must be attached to that gift. Without the truth of God's word attached to the gifts of the mind, unguarded minds will contaminate unguarded gifts. Our prayers and devotion must be Christ-centered. Christ-centered prayers and devotions that desire God to be exalted, in all that is done, will open doors that no networking or network can open. We will live our lives as witnesses of God's protection. He will guard what comes in; He will guard the canvas that He allows to be breeding ground for thoughts; and He will guard the gifts He has deposited.

Can you spare 5 more minutes?

Pillar in Practice:

The Mental

Romans 12:2 (NIV)

We must learn how to pray for our mind and why it is always necessary to do so. Our mind is, one of if not the top, priority in our prayer lives. Our mind is a place of exchange. Information goes in, it is processed, and information goes out. We are very much a product of our thoughts. According to the word of God, what we think becomes who we are.

Let's do the work!

KEY TRUTHS
1. Guard the gates to my mind.
2. Guard the grounds of my mind.
3. Guard the gifts in my mind.

GUARD MY GATES

We are products of our thoughts. Bearing this fact in mind, it is important to monitor and guard what we allow to enter into our mind. Everything that comes through our gates is a seed planted in the grounds of our mind. We have two primary gates to our mind: the eyes and the ears. It is necessary that we are proactively monitoring what we see and hear in an effort to guard our gates.

One thing I have desired of the LORD, That will I seek: That I may dwell in the house of the LORD All the days of my life, To behold the beauty of the LORD, And to inquire in His temple
-Psalm 27:4 (NIV)

Whatever you have learned or received or heard from me or seen in me- put it into practice. And the God of peace will be with you.
-Philippians 4:9 (NIV)

Therefore, everyone who hears these words of mine and puts them into practice is like a wise man that builds his house on a rock.
-Matthew 7:24 (NIV)

GUARD MY GROUNDS

Even when giving our best effort there are some things that get beyond the gates of our minds and make its way into the grounds (battlegrounds) of our mind. We should pray that God would guard our grounds so that anything that is not like Him will not be able to stay, grow, or produce fruit. Everything that get in does not have to stay in!

We are destroying speculations and every lofty thing raised up against the knowledge of God, and we are taking every thought captive to the obedience of Christ.
-2 Corinthians 10:5 (NASB)

Finally, brethren, whatsoever things are true, whatsoever things are honest, whatsoever things are just, whatsoever things are pure, whatsoever things are lovely, whatsoever things are of good report; if there be any virtue, and if there be any praise, think on these things.
-Philippians 4:8 (KJV)

But that on the good ground are they, which in an honest and good heart, having heard the word, keep it, and bring forth fruit with patience.
-Luke 8:15 (KJV)

GUARD MY GIFTS

Our mind is the place of exchange and development. Information goes in, it is developed, and it is expelled in a variety of different ways. What we speak and what we do is how the information in us is expelled. We should pray that God would guard the gifts that He has given us that begin in our minds.

Ye are the light of the world. A city that is set on a hill cannot be hid. Neither do men light a candle, and put it under a bushel, but on a candlestick; and it giveth light unto all that are in the house. Let your light so shine before men, that they may see your good works, and glorify your Father which is in heaven.
-Matthew 5:14-16 (KJV)

A man's gift makes room for him, And brings him before great men.
- Proverbs 18:16 (NKJV)

Chapter Four:
The Financial

And my God shall supply all of your needs according to His riches in glory by Christ Jesus.

-Philippians 4:19 (NKJV)

The reality that whatever we have need of is already taken care of in the economy of God is heartwarming. It's a comforting reality especially in times of struggle. There is also comfort to be found in the fact that as God has promised to supply all of our needs, our decision to prioritize His kingdom, with what He has given to us, makes us a part of the cycle of reciprocity at work. But theses priorities differ from what the world offers as the way to the stability of the kingdom. It is through prayer and meditation with God that we can come to understand the Kingdom's economics that provide us with the promise of being taken care of, but they likewise admonish us that it is more blessed to give than to receive.

Father, teach me kingdom economics...

More often than not, in this postmodern culture, the money that we earn does not make the impact in our lives nor in the world that it really should make. With so many hopes, dreams, and visions in mind, it is increasingly difficult to see these things come to life with the finances that we may have access to. The lack can often cause us to become unmotivated or discouraged by what we see if we don't remember the role of prayer in these situations. We should then pray that God would change our mindset about money. Kingdom economics suggests to us that giving produces an answered need or desire. So many times, in scripture, God challenges us to trust that if we give to the kingdom, our hands will be blessed with what we need. The widow woman, in the Old Testament, was desperate to simply care for her and her son. God sends the prophet Isaiah to her to speak a word over her, but she is commanded to feed the prophet her last before she sees the promise of the words spoken to her. Can you imagine your time in devotion and prayer, to God concerning your needs, and you have been pouring out of your spirit—the depths of your soul. All of the crying out and praying you have been doing and when God answers your prayer, *He commands your obedience before he confers your need?*

We too may find ourselves in a position of giving to the Kingdom before we see the promise of the word spoken to us. But God will ensure that when you give to the Kingdom, you are likewise blessed for the work of the Kingdom. This leads us to understanding that the primary reason God gives us resources is to fund HIS kingdom. What the widow woman provided to the prophet was a blessing to the kingdom of God and as a result, she was blessed to continue to take care of her home. This then suggests that when we prioritize God's work, He prioritizes our needs and sometimes our desires. How can this be proven? *But seek first his kingdom and His righteousness, and all these things will be given to you as well. -Matthew 6:33 (NIV).* Verse 22 of this same chapter reminds us that before we even seek the Kingdom, the Father already knows what we have need of! Kingdom economics requires spiritual strategy. And Kingdom economics says prayer is a priority!

Kingdom economics also says that everything you possess should have Kingdom Priority! Consider Nehemiah's experience: *"Furthermore I said to the king, "If it pleases the king, let letters be given to me for the governors of the region beyond the River, that they must permit me to pass through till I come to Judah, and a letter to Asaph the keeper of the king's forest, that he must give me timber to make beams for the gates of the citadel which pertains to the temple, for the city wall, and for the house that I will occupy." And the king granted them to me according to the good hand of my God upon me" -Nehemiah 2:7-8 (NKJV).* In kingdom economics, God has already ensured that things will work out in your favor. Your responsibility is to prioritize the kingdom! Nehemiah prioritized the kingdom and scripture also tells us that he did so through prayer and fasting. Our source is the kingdom!

Father, teach me to be a better steward...

Our mindset about money could be different if we understood that it is not for us to keep; it is for us to manage according to the Kingdom's agenda. If we use any other guidelines that are different from those in the

Kingdom's economy, we run the risk of diminishing the effectiveness of our resources! Let's consider an initial truth: everything we have belongs to God! *The earth is the Lord's and the fullness thereof –the world and they that dwell therein -Psalm 24:1(NKJV).* What a privilege it is to have a hand in managing what belongs to the one who owns it all! And our perspective of management has to be much different from the world's standard of management. *"The rich rules over the poor, And the borrower is servant to the lender" -Proverbs 22:7(NKJV).* Solomon's wisdom suggests that those who rule in the earth, take first for themselves and then rule over those who have much less than them. It's a thwarted economy. But we who are children of God have not been called to such.

The economy of God is personal and personable! It's personal in a sense that we all have individual mandates on our lives which should be used to edify the kingdom of God. It's personable in a sense that the gifts we possess are also to be a blessing to others and be used as tools to draw those, who don't know Jesus as Lord and savior, into the Kingdom family. In other words, the economy of God is not simply about what makes dollars and cents. Like any system, people are also important to the economy. And the truth is that being better stewards of the Kingdom's agenda also makes us better stewards of the Kingdom's creation. *"As each one has received a special gift, employ it in serving one another as good stewards of the manifold grace of God" -1 Peter 4:10 (NASB).* Everyone has been given a gift—some of us possess gifts. Whatever our lot, we are responsible for using these gifts to serve one another! We glorify God in how we treat the gifts He has placed in us. We also glorify God in how we use the gifts He's placed around us. What a shame for us to abuse the gift of people and only value the material gifts.

Ultimately, the product or the fruit of a life that is committed to be a better steward, in the economy of God, will experience God allowing all things to fall into place according to His will for our lives. *Commit your works to the Lord and your plans will be established. -Proverbs 16:3 (NASB)*. This suggests to us that our prayers cannot be ones tailored to completing our own agendas. Our time in mediation and prayer should not be inundated with our own plans and everything that we want to do. In prayer, asking God to make me a better steward presses upon me the need to surrender my will. The will of the Lord must be priority in Kingdom economics. In presenting ourselves to God, we surrender our own wills to see His will be done! Our Christ-centered prayers will produce Christ-centered lives that change the world!

Father, teach me how to have multiple streams of income…

When we have the progress of the Kingdom in mind and on our hearts, we should pray that God would continue to increase us so that we may be able to increase the Kingdom. With more resources, we increase our ability to help others. Our lives are not lived to simply pay bills. God has provided us with gifts, talents, skills, and intellect that are to be used to helped sustain our daily needs. But the same are to be used to advance the assignments that have been attached to our lives. And it is difficult for us to carry out the assignments from God on our lives when we are not financially prepared for the shifts that happen so spontaneously. What God has placed in us gives us the ability to establish multiple streams of income that we can use to glorify Him!

God presents us with provision in pursuing His work and His kingdom—His way. *"Now may He who supplies seed to the sower, and bread for food, supply and multiply the seed you have sown and increase the fruits of your righteousness, while you are enriched in everything for all liberality, which causes thanksgiving through us to God" -2 Corinthians 9:10-11 (NIV).* The Apostle Paul suggests that we are blessed to be a blessing! And when we are willing to release what we possess to see good happen to others and glory go to God, we put ourselves in a position to always be blessed! God increases and multiplies what we have more than we could even imagine. And the words of the song are true, "You can't beat God giving no matter how you try. And just as sure as you are living, and the Lord is in heaven on high. The more you give, the more He gives to you, but keep on giving because it's really true. That you can't beat God's giving, no matter how you try."

And out of the ground the Lord God made every tree grow that is pleasant to the sight and good for food. The tree of life was also in the midst of the garden, and the tree of the knowledge of good and evil. Now a river went out of Eden to water the garden, and from there it parted and became four riverheads -Genesis 2:9-10 (NKJV). The economy of God is as real now as it was in the garden. He was provider in the garden, and He is provider in our current reality. He was supplier in the garden and today He still supplies our needs every day. We have to be Kingdom-minded because the disconnect does not come at the ability of God to provide; the disconnect we experience comes from our inability to fully trust and believe.

Father, teach me to rebuke the devourer...

When you are a tither/gracious giver, you can ask God to stop things that cause your finances to hemorrhage. There are always things in life that will attempt to rob you of your resources to stunt Kingdom growth. If you are a giver, you can and should pray God's divine protection over your finances. *"And I will rebuke the devourer for your sakes, So that he will not destroy the fruit of your ground, Nor shall the vine fail to bear fruit for you in the field," Says The Lord of Hosts..." -Malachi 3:11 (NKJV).* The tithe presents an opportunity for God to bless you for trusting Him with just a portion of what He has already given to you! Verse 9 also admonishes believers to ensure that they prioritize the tithe for the kingdom of God. Believers are responsible for sewing into the Kingdom of God and sowing produces a harvest! Many times, we are looking for our harvest to be financial—almost like an investment. The reality is that there are other ways in which God makes the tithe beneficial to our lives. Tithing not only releases fruit to us but tithing also breaks curses in our lives. We are capable of rebuking the adversary when we are obedient to the will and work of our Lord.

Can you spare 5 more minutes?

Pillar in Practice:
The Financial

And my God shall supply all of your needs according to
His riches in glory by Christ Jesus.

-Philippians 4:19 (NKJV)

It is imperative to KNOW that God is concerned about your needs. Being convinced that God is concerned about each of our needs, should change the vantage point that we pray from, and it should change our mindset and the language that we use when praying for our needs.

I have been young, and now am old; Yet I have not seen
the righteous forsaken, Nor his descendants begging
bread.
-Psalms 37:25 NASB

Let's do the work!

KEY TRUTHS

1. Teach me Kingdom economics.
2. Teach me to be a better steward.
3. Teach me how to have multiple streams of income.
4. Teach me to rebuke the devourer.

TEACH ME KINGDOM ECONOMICS

More often than not, in the postmodern culture that we live in, the money that we earn does not make the impact in our life nor in the world that it really should make. We should pray that God would change our mindset about money. We must understand that the primary reason God gives us resources is to fund HIS kingdom.

But seek first his kingdom and his righteousness, and all these things will be given to you as well.
-Matthew 6:33 (NIV)

If it pleases the king, let letters be given to me for the governors of the region beyond the River, that they must permit me to pass through till I come to Judah, and a letter to Asaph the keeper of the king's forest, that he must give me timber to make beams for the gates of the citadel which pertains to the temple, for the city wall, and for the house that I will occupy." And the king granted them to me according to the good hand of my God upon me.

-Nehemiah 2:7-8 (NKJV)

Everything that you possess should be have Kingdom Priority!

TEACH ME TO BE A BETTER STEWARD

Our mindset about money might be different if we understood that it is not for us to keep, it is for us to manage according to the Kingdom's agenda. If we use any other guidelines that are different from those in the Kingdom's economy, we run the risk of diminishing the effectiveness of our resources.

"The rich rules over the poor, And the borrower is servant to the lender"
-Proverbs 22:7(NKJV)

As each one has received a special gift, employ it in serving one another as good stewards of the manifold grace of God.
-1 Peter 4:10 (NASB)

Commit your works to the Lord and your plans will be established.
-Proverbs 16:3 (NASB)

TEACH ME HOW TO HAVE MULTIPLE STREAMS OF INCOME

When you have the progress of the Kingdom in your mind and on your heart, we should pray that God would continue to increase us so that we may be able to increase the Kingdom. The more resources that we have increases our ability to help others.

"Now may He who supplies seed to the sower, and bread for food, supply and multiply the seed you have sown and increase the fruits of your righteousness, while you are enriched in everything for all liberality, which causes thanksgiving through us to God"
-2 Corinthians 9:10-11 (NIV).

And out of the ground the Lord God made every tree grow that is pleasant to the sight and good for food. The tree of life was also in the midst of the garden, and the tree of the knowledge of good and evil. Now a river went out of Eden to water the garden, and from there it parted and became four riverheads
-Genesis 2:9-10 (NKJV).

TEACH ME HOW TO REBUKE THE DEVOURER

When you are a tither/gracious giver, you can ask God to stop things that cause your finances to hemorrhage. There are always things in life that will try to rob you of your resources in an attempt to stunt Kingdom growth. If you are a giver, you can and should pray God's divine protection over your finances.

And I will rebuke the devourer for your sakes, So that he will not destroy the fruit of your ground, Nor shall the vine fail to bear fruit for you in the field," Says The Lord of Hosts...
-Malachi 3:11 (NKJV).

Chapter Five:

The Emotional

Above all else, guard your heart, for everything you do flows from it.

-Proverbs 4:23 (NIV)

We have explored so many areas of wellness for the believer and emotional health is not the least of these. Matters of the heart should matter to us! It is time that we pray for "Heart Health." Physicians seem to have synchronized reports that suggest what we can do to preserve our natural heart health which include: a controlled portion size, a limit on unhealthy fats and cholesterol, and planning ahead. These principles apply to the emotional health of the heart as well. As a matter of fact, many of the previously discussed areas are affected stemming from the emotional well-being of us all. Solomon provides us with wisdom suggesting that when the heart is not well, it puts other areas of our lives at risk. And whether we'd like to admit it or not, simply being *too blessed to be stressed and too anointed to be disappointed* is not the care that we should seek. It's also true that our physical hearts are just as important to the spirituality of our hearts.

We explored the importance of taking care of our temples in "The Physical" and now we are focusing on the spiritual heart as well as the physical heart.

Father, help me to keep my heart with all diligence...

The heart is of a perishable nature-- it is not unbreakable, impenetrable or bulletproof. There are many things that can scar us emotionally and cause us long-term damage. Asking God to keep our hearts means we are asking Him to keep watch over, protect and preserve them. And we must pray that God would empower us to be vigilant and protective of our hearts. The truth is that our spiritual maturity and emotional health are linked. Paul suggests to the church at Ephesus, *"Put on the whole armor of God, that ye may be able to stand against the wiles of the devil. For we wrestle not against flesh and blood, but against principalities, against powers, against the rulers of the darkness of this world, against spiritual wickedness in high places" - Ephesians 6:11-12 (KJV).*

Our spiritual heart health will surely experience spiritual warfare. This is the battle between right and wrong—good and evil. And these are issues that can penetrate the heart and cause us damage if we are not prepared with the tools given to us by God. It is the word of God and the prayers of the saints that will help protect the heart from the casualties of this struggle. Spiritual warfare will present itself in situations and through people, but the Lord requires us to see past the distraction directly in front of us. The word of God suggests that what we are at war with is in the spirit realm. And our weapons cannot be carnal. This is why our devotion and prayer to God is so important. It has to be a critical part of our day. We have no idea what we are stepping into once we step out of our homes on any given day. Worse than this, some of us don't know what we will wake up to in our own homes on any given day.

This battle can cause physical stress and harm to our hearts if not properly handled. And our protection and healing won't be found in relying on our own strengths. God is our divine protector and healer. This is kingdom practice given by a divine physician. We must rely on the power of God to protect our hearts.

Father, help me to control my portion size...

Just as with food, when we eat too much, it causes us to be lethargic, slow, heavy, and sometimes it leads to sickness and disease. So, it is spiritually: if we take on more than we should emotionally, it can slow down the progression of our lives. We are often overwhelmed because we overload. Countless scriptures and songs of encouragement suggest to us that our responsibility is to acknowledge and trust God's ability to share our load and carry us through whatever it is we may have to face in life. We mess up when we attempt to handle everything alone and God never expected us to do this. Why overwhelm yourself when you've been invited to give your situations, problems and troubles to the One who can make all things new? When we pray, we should ask God to help us balance what we take on and what we have to put out.

And what does emotional balance look like for the believer? An unbalanced believer wants to work through the symptoms of an issue but doesn't like to deal with the actual problem causing the issue. How does this affect my portion size? The problem can be singular in nature, but the symptoms can be many. When we don't deal with the emotional problems of our lives, we invite the symptoms to take residence. And this is what the unstable and unbalanced believer experiences when we deny ourselves the opportunity to *cast our cares on Him—He cares for us.*

Father, help me to limit unhealthy fats and cholesterol...

Fats are only a small part of the larger good. It is when they are taken in too frequently that they do more harm than good. Digesting the fats on certain food can be harmful, still, that doesn't mean the whole is bad--only that part. This is relative to emotional health as well. Things and people that are good for us but even they too carry a small bad part. We must be prayerful that we don't take on too much of the "fat" from them. We should pray that God would help us to not overload ourselves with the unhealthy things around us.

This list could be endless: people, work, conversations, television, and so much more and these are all environmental variables that are a part of our everyday lives but when abused can wreak havoc on our lives. The limits are necessary because if we are not careful, we will find ourselves in situations that make our environments priority over our relationship with God. We can even consider prayer that promotes us not prioritizing ourselves over our relationship with God. There are times when too much of us is a bad thing. Is it too much care of one's self? Not at all. Sometimes, it's too much of a poor attitude, too much of a pity party, too much of our own negative thoughts that damages our emotional well-being.

Too much of unhealthy fats and cholesterol cause blockage to the heart. This is what leads to heart attacks in the physical heart. What is blocking the arteries, vessels, or pathways to your emotional health? What is it that you have hoarded and refused to release to the Lord that is putting your emotional heart health at risk of causing the death of a part of your heart?

Father, help me to plan ahead...

The issues of life flow from my heart. Armed with this knowledge, I should pray that God would help me to plan ahead by filtering what I allow into my heart. And my heart cannot be any good to anyone else if I am not good to it. God requires my heart to love His people and If I allow it to keep being abused, by me or anyone else, it becomes incapacitated and toxic toward the same people that God wants me to use my heart to love.

Imagine attempting to assist someone with a damaged heart that you refuse to get repaired. Perhaps we consider this to be a form of spiritual malpractice. Not addressing the issues of our hearts or relying on God's word to take care of our hearts implies that we believe we can fix ourselves. But the word of God remains true: *"Trust in the Lord with all thine heart; and lean not unto thine own understanding. In all thy ways acknowledge him, and he shall direct thy paths" -Proverbs 3:5(KJV).*

And it shouldn't take an act of tragedy to make us prioritize our emotional health. *Plan ahead!* We can prevent the spiritual heart attack and practice talking to our creator. *Plan ahead!* Our communication to Him should not just be about what we need and want. This is where many of us make mistakes because we wait to talk to the Lord when we stand in need. This is the difference between being proactive and reactive. Plan ahead and stay in communication with God! *The prudent sees the evil and hides himself, But the naive go on, and are punished for it. -Proverbs 22:3(NIV).* The prudent are not paranoid; they are proactive. The prudent are able to stay a few steps ahead of things because their solace is in God the Father knowing that He is before all things, in all things and sovereign over all things.

Planning ahead makes us good stewards of what God has already given to us. We plan because we live in a world that is often unpredictable and is incredibly spontaneous. We have to trust God because He is the same God who causes whatever we experience to work out for our good!

Can you spare 5 more minutes?

Pillar in Practice:

The Emotional

Above all else, guard your heart, for everything you do flows from it.

-Proverbs 4:23 (NIV)

It is time that we pray for "Heart Health." According to a recent report in a medical journal, there are a few things that we can do to preserve our natural heart health. These include controlling your portion size, limiting unhealthy fats and cholesterol, and planning ahead.

Let's do the work!

KEY TRUTHS
    1. Help me to keep my heart with all diligence.
    2. Help me to control my portion size.
    3. Help me to limit unhealthy fats and cholesterol.
    4. Help me to plan ahead

HELP ME TO KEEP MY HEART

To keep my heart means to keep watch over, to protect, to preserve. The heart is of a perishable nature. It is not unbreakable, impenetrable, or bulletproof. There are things that can scar us emotionally and cause us long-term damage. We must pray that God would empower us to be vigilant and protective of our hearts.

Put on the whole armor of God, that ye may be able to stand against the wiles of the devil. For we wrestle not against flesh and blood, but against principalities, against powers, against the rulers of the darkness of this world, against spiritual wickedness in high places.
-Ephesians 6:11-12 (KJV)

HELP ME CONTROL MY PORTION SIZE

Just as with food, when we eat too much, it causes us to be lethargic, slow, heavy, and sometimes it leads to sickness and disease and so it is spiritually. If we take on more than we should emotionally, it can slow the progression of our lives. We are often overwhelmed because we overload. When we pray, we should ask God to help us balance what we take on and what we have to put out.

HELP ME TO LIMIT UNHEALTHY FAT

Fats are a small part of the larger whole. Digesting the fats on certain food can be harmful, but that doesn't mean that the whole is bad-- only that part. Things and people that are good for us even carry a small bad part and we must be prayerful that we don't take on too much of the "fat" from them. We should pray that God would help us to not overload ourselves with the unhealthy things around us.

HELP ME TO PLAN AHEAD

The issues of life flow from my heart. Armed with this knowledge, I should pray that God would help me to plan ahead by filtering what I allow into my heart. God uses my heart to love His people and If I allow it to keep being abused, it becomes incapacitated and toxic toward the same people that God wants me to use my heart to love.

Trust in the Lord with all thine heart; and lean not unto thine own understanding. In all thy ways acknowledge him, and he shall direct thy paths.
-Proverbs 3:5(KJV).

Prayers That Work

Be careful for nothing; but in everything by prayer and supplication with thanksgiving let your requests be made known unto God. And the peace of God, which passeth all understanding, shall keep your hearts and minds through Christ Jesus.

- Philippians 4:16-17 (KJV)

The Danger of Unacknowledged Doubt...

You cannot conquer what you do not confront! One of the foundational principles of prayer is an unshakeable resolve that God exists and that He rewards those who seek Him. Doubt is to prayer what tiny holes are to a boat. It will not sink it immediately, but it will ultimately. We must conquer doubt in order to unleash the unfiltered power of prayer:

- *Proverbs 23:7-For as a man thinks in his heart, so is he... (A life filled with doubt, is a life filled with need.)*
- *Proverbs 16:3-Commit your works to the Lord, and your thoughts will be established.* (Doubt displaces our blessed position when we fail to or refuse to commit our works to the Lord.)
- *Matthew 6:33-But seek first the kingdom of God and His righteousness, and all these things shall be added to you.* (Proper prioritization of purpose will cause doubt to dissipate and help you to see your prayers answered.)

<u>Make Your Request Known...</u>
(But in everything by PRAYER...)

In everything, without exclusion, we are to petition God especially regarding circumstances that cause anxiety. This means that we are to make a formal request to the creator of the universe in every circumstance we face:

- *1 John 5:14,15-Now this is the confidence that we have in Him, that if we ask anything*

78

according to His will, He hears us. And if we know that He hears us, whatever we ask, we know that we have the petitions that we have asked of Him.

- *Ephesians 6:18-Praying always with all prayer and supplication in the spirit, being watchful to this end with all perseverance and supplication for all saints.*

The Entreaty...
(...by prayer and SUPPLICATION with thanksgiving...)

A supplication is typically associated with an urgent solicitation based on need. Paired here with THANKSGIVING, it paints the picture of a negotiation. I can come to God and plead the case of my needs being met based on my positioning with Him and my presentations to Him. To the negotiating table I bring: My need, His word, His will, our relationship, and thanksgiving.

- *James 5:13-Is anyone among you in trouble? Let him pray. Is anyone cheerful? Let him sing psalms.*

- *Proverbs 15:8-The sacrifice of the wicked is an abomination to God, but the prayer of the upright is His delight.*
- *Psalms 102:17-He will respond to the prayer of the destitute; He will not despise their plea.*
- *1 Timothy 2:1-Therefore I exhort first of all that supplications, prayers, intercessions, and giving of thanks be made for all men...*

Make Your Requests...

(...let your REQUESTS be made known unto God...)

Making your requests known to God in no way implies that He is not already fully aware of what it is that you need. There is not a single thing that escapes His attention. When we tell God about our specific needs, it is the act of releasing our cares, anxiety, and concerns into the capable hands of our Father.

- *Psalm 55:22-Cast your burden on the Lord, and He shall sustain you; He shall never permit the righteous to be moved.*
- *1 Peter 5:7-Casting all your cares upon Him, for He cares for you.*

Praying in 3-D

*And Jesus rebuked the demon, and it came out of him;
and the child was cured from that very hour. Then the
disciples came to Jesus privately and said, "Why could
we not cast it out? So Jesus said to them, "Because of
your unbelief; for assuredly, I say to you, if you have
faith as a mustard seed, you will say to this mountain,
"move from here to there." and it will move; and nothing
will be impossible for you. However, this kind does not
go out except by prayer and fasting."
-Matthew 17:18-21(NKJV)*

Faith: The First Dimension...

In order to have any reasonable expectations in
praying, our prayers must be rooted in faith. Faith is the
precursor for prayer.

- *Hebrews 11:6-But without faith it is impossible to please Him, for they that come to God must believe that He is, and that He is a rewarder of those who diligently seek him.*
- *Romans 10:17-So then faith comes from hearing, and hearing through the word of God*
- *2 Corinthians 5:7-For we walk by faith and not by sight.*

Fasting: The Second Dimension...

Fasting is one of three spiritual disciplines. Praying, Giving, & Fasting are the three disciplines that every believer should be diligently looking to maintain. Biblical fasting is abstaining from either all foods or certain foods for a specified period of time while consecrating yourself. (Daniel 1:16-20)

- It's not the fast, it's the feature. (It's a display of discipline & restraint.
- When you set yourself apart for God, He'll set you apart from men.
- God is not speeding up the process; He's speeding up your progress in the process. (You're going to go farther faster.)

Prayer: The Third Dimension...

Prayer is the real battlefield of the world. God, the angels, the hosts of heaven all look down upon prayers that are being made. Prayer is the battlefield where decisive events of time, history, and future are tipped toward one direction or another. (Acts 12:5-16)

- Prayer impacts time. (Acts 12:3)
- Prayer in community impacts people. (Acts 12:6)
- Prayer stirs heaven. (Acts 12:7)
- Prayer provides instructions. (Acts 12: 7-9)
- Prayer opens closed doors. (Acts 12:10)

65146105R00052